The MALADY of AMERICAN CHRISTIANITY

How Congregations Often Fail to Teach the Church's Main Purpose What the Commandments have to do with it.

Franklin L. Grepke

WESTBOW
PRESS®
A DIVISION OF THOMAS NELSON
& ZONDERVAN

This book is a work of non-fiction. Unless otherwise noted, the author and the publisher make no explicit guarantees as to the accuracy of the information contained in this book and in some cases, names of people and places have been altered to protect their privacy.

WestBow Press books may be ordered through booksellers or by contacting:

WestBow Press
A Division of Thomas Nelson & Zondervan
1663 Liberty Drive
Bloomington, IN 47403
www.westbowpress.com
844-714-3454

Scripture quotations are from The ESV® Bible (The Holy Bible, English Standard Version®), copyright © 2001 by Crossway, a publishing ministry of Good News Publishers. Used by permission. All rights reserved.

ISBN: 978-1-6642-2879-5 (sc)
ISBN: 978-1-6642-2878-8 (hc)
ISBN: 978-1-6642-2877-1 (e)

Library of Congress Control Number: 2021906081

Print information available on the last page.

WestBow Press rev. date: 4/6/2021

ACKNOWLEDGEMENTS

I want to thank Dr. Kent Hunter for his support, encouragement, and help in editing this manuscript. His experience as an author of several books like _Who Broke My Church, Restoring Civility_, and others has encouraged me with this project.

I want to thank my wife, Joann, for her encouragement and insights she has added to this book. Her devotion to be a life-long learner is an inspiration to me. Thank you, I love you.

Thanks to Karla Keesler, a friend, and the Administrative Assistant at my church, for her precision and careful editing and documentation of the book.

I thank my nephew, Neil Grepke, Director of Christ Academy and Theology Department at Faith Lutheran High School in Las Vegas, NV, for his precision and critique of the grammar and Theology. His suggestions helped me to refocus sentence structure and make the book clearer.

CONTENTS

PREFACE

The Malady of American Christianity is based on my observation of a threefold value system that many church goers embrace. While they may say their priorities in life are God first, family second, and country last; by actions and words their actual priorities in life are country (flag) first, family second, and God third. I will share my personal observations, biblical references, personal experiences and quotes from other authors. You will read shocking statements and stories. Keep an eye out for those statements.

The basic outline is in Exodus 20, the Ten Commandments. All quotes of the Commandments are from Martin Luther's Small Catechism. It is my hope to bring fresh insights about how the Ten Commandments and the purpose of the Church apply to the daily walk of the Christian. God has a specific plan for how the world is to be reached for Christ. This purpose includes that Jesus came to die for the sins of all people, to bring salvation through His life, death, and resurrection, and to model how to make followers or disciples.

Writing has always been a challenge for me. My heart is on these pages. It is my expression of love, faith, joy, forgiveness, and hope.

Church
When used with a capital "C" it is referring to the Church universal.

church
When used with a small "c" it is referring to congregations.

INTRODUCTION

"For by this time you ought to be teachers, you need someone to teach you again the basic principles of the oracles of God, you need milk, not solid food, for everyone who lives on milk is unskilled in the word of righteousness, since he is a child. But solid food is for the mature, for those who have their powers of discernment trained by constant practice to distinguish good from evil". [1]

Discernment can be frustrating for those who are gifted to have it. It can be a struggle to decide how to use this ability to help rather than hinder others in their faith. If words are chosen in the wrong way, they can offend. If they are spoken in a better way, they can encourage. They build up faith. My aim is to build you up in your faith. However, if some things written here cause a conscience issue, I pray it will lead to repentance and restoration.

There are some experiences worth sharing. God has gifted me with a heart and passion for seeing people's lives changed by Christ. It is such joy to see the lights in their eyes when they know their sins are forgiven and they have a new future with God. Here are some examples: Does it matter to Brownie at International Harvester or the taxicab driver in Nigeria that I shared Jesus with them? Only God knows. Does it matter that the children I taught preconfirmation classes to in Milwaukee made me burst with pride when they told their stories about their relationship

---

[1] Heb. 5:12-14 (English Standard Version; all subsequent citations are from this version).

with Jesus? Only God knows. Does it matter to those adults who learned how to tell their stories about Jesus when I taught them how to share their faith? Only God knows. Will it matter to the older adults in hospitals and nursing homes with whom I have shared God's Word and prayers? Only God knows.

Do you know your purpose? A broader question is: Do you know the purpose of a church? Kent Hunter, a consultant of congregations, asks members to fill out a questionnaire answering their understanding of the purpose of the church. It consists of four descriptions: (1) to teach people how to live the golden rule; (2) to be the moral backbone of society; (3) to make disciples; and (4) to provide a place of fellowship, to share God's love with one another. Of course, each of these choices may have some merit, but only one is correct. Over several years, compiling data, he discovered, only 34% of church members chose the correct answer. This means that 66% did not know. What about you? Would you choose the correct answer? For now, I will let you think about that question.

Earlier in my life I worked at International Harvester Company in Fort Wayne, Indiana. At work I was involved with a group who studied the Bible every day during lunch break. This was when I learned about the mission of the church. We not only studied the Bible, but we *Do you know the purpose of the church?* shared it with our fellow employees. Our group was small when we began, but as we influenced and shared about Jesus with our fellow employees, the study groups grew and multiplied throughout the plant. There were no denominational barriers. We accepted each person and agreed that we did not want to hinder our study with denominational distractions that caused problems. Our central focus was Jesus. Our aim was to share Him with others. God placed His call on my heart, and I was led to enroll in Bible college. Then the plant closed and many of those in our study group also went on to ministry. It was at Bible college; the purpose of the Church was reaffirmed for me.

Here is the purpose of the Church: "And Jesus came and said to them, all authority in heaven and on earth has been given to me. Go therefore and make disciples of all nations, baptizing them in the name of the Father and the Son and the Holy Spirit, teaching them to observe all that I have commanded you, to the end of the age."[2]

These words of Jesus have often been minimized by churches. Some emphasize something different. Some congregational leaders limit disciple making to baptizing and classes to join their denomination. Yet these efforts are only a part of the process of making disciples. Baptizing and early training in the Christian faith for the purpose of leading to "church membership" is only the beginning. In bringing us to faith by the Holy Spirit, our Triune God, desires for us to journey with Him our whole life, with Him in the lead. An active Christian life involves growing in intimate knowledge of His will, discerning what He wants and His ways, and following "His footsteps." The entire Bible is a salvation story! The Ten Commandments from the start were God's gifts to His people to guide us in our journey with Him. All of Scripture is history of salvation. The Gospel, the "Good News," is the golden thread throughout. Scriptures says, "For God so loved the world,

Some congregational leaders limit disciple making to baptizing and classes to join their denomination.

---

[2] Matthew 28:18-20. (ESV)

that he gave his only Son, that whoever believes in him should not perish but have eternal life."[3] This gospel ties us to the life, death, and resurrection of Jesus. His basic commandments or instructions for the journey are also illustrated throughout the Old and New Testament. Our loving Father offers us the best guidance for a joy-filled life with him.

For that joy-filled life, we look to Jesus' model. People often miss Jesus' key statement, "teaching them to observe all that I have commanded you."[4] The model and methods Jesus taught include a relational one-on-one with His disciples. He did not teach a program. He did not teach a seminary apologetics course. He was the model of obedience to His and Our Father. He spent three years demonstrating and teaching what it meant to be His follower. This was their challenge. The model is not normal. It is not taught in a seminary.

> *The model and methods Jesus taught include a relational one-on-one with His disciples. He did not teach a program.*

After Bible college I served at a central city church in Detroit, Michigan. Pastor Kent Hunter was teaching members of the church Evangelism Explosion, developed by Dr. D. James Kennedy, Pastor of Coral Ridge Presbyterian Church in Florida. For me to begin teaching this course, the church sent me to Coral Ridge to receive this same training. The best fundamental principle of discipling I learned was the six growth steps for modeling discipleship. Kent Hunter writes a description of those steps in his book, *Restoring Civility*.

---

[3] John 3:16 (ESV)
[4] Matthew 28:20 (ESV)

Step one. Want to hang out with me? Come with me on hospital visits. Step two. I do/you watch. Watch as I listen intently and apply God's word to the person's need. Step three. I do/you help. When the time is right read some appropriate Bible selections. Step four. You do/I help. You lead the listening and conversation while I offer input as needed. Step five. You do/I watch. You are taking the lead. We discuss how it went afterwards. Step six. This step is about letting go. It is called respected independence.

Each of these steps is intended to model ways and means to do and serve in ministry.

There were two young men, Alan, and Dan, who were members of that central city church. One was an attorney. The other was an engineer. They both participated in our evangelism training classes. They both concluded that they wanted to become better equipped for ministry, so we implemented a ministry training model to further equip them. The first step was to come on hospital and shut-in visits. My wife Joann was good at this part of mentoring. For some time, we continued to give Alan and Dan this ongoing training process. Included in the training were reading assignments. Different books were assigned as well as Scripture for edification. We gave them worship participation experience; things like reading the lessons, assisting with communion, and offering personal testimonies. We took them through the six steps. Soon they were convinced that God was calling them to full-time ministry. Both went to the seminary. Dan was trained in Hispanic ministry and now teaches Mexican citizens in Mexico how to be pastors and deaconesses. Alan was called to serve in a congregation as a pastor.

This model of discipleship breaks the mold for a church. It transforms a church from a religious institution into a training center for sending apprenticed disciples into ministry. A congregation's aim should be to follow Jesus' teaching, using His model for making disciples.

Finally, a fresh insight for me: An incredibly significant and important part of discipling is to lead church members toward a greater knowledge and understanding of the Ten Commandments. As we live out our lives as disciples, we will also follow the laws of God—all by the guidance of the Holy Spirit.

The law is still our mirror, our boundary, and our guide as we follow Christ. The mirror should always show us who we really are, warts and all. It should lead us to repentance and humility.

The boundaries are God's way of keeping us on the right path. Like little children who want to run loose and do their own thing without supervision, we need restrictions. I taught my children about the corral theory. This meant that I expected them to stay within the perimeters of the corral, which included good morals, love toward others, and obeying God's laws as well as civil laws. As they grew and matured, I expanded the corral and gave them more space and freedom. Finally, I learned I could trust them, and at that point, then I could release them.

Discipling is to lead church members toward a greater knowledge and understanding of the Ten Commandments.

Finally, the law should be our guide, enabled by the power of the Holy Spirit. The third use of the law is a guide. Social media reflects that many church goers have little or no regard for the commandments. It is sad that there are so many abuses when it comes to one's relationship with Christ. Many Christians today seem to believe the commandments cannot be kept anyway, so why even try. As humans we cannot keep the commandments perfectly. However, Jesus Christ can and does keep them. That is why your focus should be on the cross. Jesus is your guide with the Holy Spirit leading you on your walk. If you stumble in your walk, grace: God's Riches At Christ's Expense, restores our walk with Jesus. He keeps His promise of never forsaking us or leaving us without guidance. It is why He gave us the Holy Spirit. This is the reason I have included one of the commandments in each of the following chapters. It is why I invite you to come with me on this journey as we focus on the meaning behind each commandment.

CHAPTER ONE

HEART TREASURES

"You shall have no other gods ...."[5] *What does this mean?*

Answer: We should fear, love, and trust in God above all things.[6]

---

[5] Exodus 20:3 (ESV)

[6] Luther's Small Catechism, all subsequent citations are from the Lutheran Confessions, Concordia Publishing House Second Edition. Scriptures quoted are from the ESV (English Standard Version)

Jesus says, "For where your treasure is, there your heart will be also."[7] Matthew 6:21 describes a *spiritual heart condition.* Things like cars and houses are not bad. Yet our hearts can be bad. A couple of years ago I suffered a heart attack. Why? Because I ignored the signs that something was wrong. All the pains and discomfort, the shortness of breath, I wrote them off as indigestion. One Sunday morning, I was getting dressed for church when things went bad. Pow! Like a bolt of lightning, I was in pain, and the pressure in my chest was like I had never experienced before. (Like Redd Foxx on *Sanford and Son*, I was having the "big one.") Long story short, my wife took me to the hospital, and they put in a stent. Although this was a physical heart problem, the analogy can be applied to the spiritual condition of your congregation. Ignoring something does not make it go away. Ignoring the spiritual health of your church causes many challenges: stagnation, few new members, few people growing in Bible study, and a maintenance mindset with no mission.

A subtle influence occurs when church members ignore the fundamental teachings about what it means to follow Christ. This does not imply they are spiritual "failures." It means the mirror they are looking in is very smoky. The law is still relevant. It points us to the cross. The mirror of the law helps us look at where our heart is in relationship with God, and the boundaries of God's law keep

> *Ignoring the spiritual health of your church causes many challenges: stagnation, few new members, few people growing in Bible study, and a maintenance mindset with no mission.*

---

[7] Matthew 6:21 (ESV)

us in line. If this is not the case, the church is nothing more than an institution. It becomes a religious organization that makes "members" not disciples.

Michael Foss writes, "I have been guilty of the Membership Model for recruitment in ministry. In the Membership Model, the first and often only question is: Are they breathing? The tragedy of this method of recruiting for the work of God through the church is that it diminishes both the person and purpose to which we call people."[8]

The church is not a social club. It is an equipping center for nurturing and growing Christians into mature disciples. People are called to use their giftedness in acts of ministry and service. Obstacles, like traditions and old ways of doing things, get in the way. I used to eat foods that were not healthy for me. Sometimes I still do. As a result, cholesterol became a problem. Eating the wrong things were the habits that later caused problems.

The First Commandment is clear. We should have no other gods. That even includes traditions. Which reminds me of the time a member at a congregation, we attended, stood up in a meeting and waved the hymnal, saying it was the very word of God.

Methods of recruitment, church practices, anything we place as a priority over our relationship with God is or can become a god. Even time can become a distraction to our relationship with Christ. People say, "I do not have time for going to church." "I do not have time to attend Bible class." "I only get time on Sunday to do my fishing, golfing, or hunting." These can be selfish sinful and unhealthy conditions of the heart. Time becomes a god that stems from the sin of selfishness. We place ourselves above God.

---

[8] Michael Foss, *From Members to Disciples*, Nashville, TN Abingdon Press, 2007, p,35

Narcissistic individuals think more highly of themselves than they do of others. Their focus is aimed at pleasing themselves. They love the attention and accolades they receive. They become their own god.

In 1525 Martin Luther wrote about the church in Saxony, Germany. He described its condition. It could be said that he wrote about a heart condition. Yet it is also an "ignorance issue." Luther writes,

> "The deplorable, miserable condition which I discovered lately, when I, too, was a visitor, has forced and urged me to prepare this Catechism, or Christian doctrine, in this small, plain, simple form. Mercy! Good God! What manifold misery I beheld! The common people...have no knowledge whatever of Christian doctrine, and alas! Many pastors are altogether incapable and incompetent to teach. Nevertheless, all maintain that they are Christians...Yet they cannot recite the Lord's Prayer, or the Creed, or the Ten Commandments, they live like dumb brutes and irrational swine."[9]

This description could fit some pastors today. They may not lack in doctrine and systematic theology, as Luther describes, but they have never learned how to make "apprentice followers" of Jesus Christ who become disciples and in turn make other disciples. Their seminary training did not equip them. Their focus is more on shepherd/teacher.

---

[9] Gerhard Bente, *The Lutheran Confessions, 156. Concordia Publishing House*

It is necessary to define what a disciple is because most members do not know. Some pastors know what it means to make disciples, but many do not. A dictionary definition calls disciples, learners, followers, devotees.[10] Each of these dictionary definitions imply much more than first perceived. There is a commitment I observe about Christians who are serious about following Christ. They are lifelong learners. The Bible is their first resource for growing in knowledge and understanding of their purpose. You will see they also love to read Christian books. Discipleship is a process.

Quoting Ephesians 4:12-13, Joann Grepke writes in her master's project, "discipleship is the process of maturing until we measure up to Christ, our standard." "The Greek word for disciple "mathetes" means more than a pupil or learner, but a devotee who accepts the instruction given to him/her and makes it one's rule of conduct. A disciple spends time with and follows his teacher."[11]

I have tried to encourage the pastors I have served with. As a lay person or elder, I have urged them to embrace the training of select members to become apprentices, much like we did at the church in Detroit. The proverbial brushoff is, "I am too busy." There is a principle I learned in the retail business. It was that one was trained to fill the shoes of every person's job in the business. Ultimately, the goal was to work yourself out of your job. Then you could move on to a more responsible job. Why don't these principles apply to the local congregation? They are not evil, or

I want to be fair about the training pastors get.

---

[10] Webster's New World Dictionary, Fourth Edition

[11] A Discipleship Curriculum for Reframing Aging, Joann Grepke p.1,9,10. Quote from Ephesians is from Voices of Faith 1998, World Pub based on God's Word to the Nations. Greek definition is from Zodhiates 919

bad, simply because the secular world embraces them. If they were evil Jesus would not have told His disciples to "Come, follow me."[12] Jesus worked himself out of His earthly job and left it in the hands of twelve uneducated men who turned the world upside down. What a God we have! What a plan He has!

I want to be fair about the training pastors get. I have observed there are two types of pastors. There are equippers and shepherds. I believe this is a spiritual dynamic. God has gifted each believer with a different view about their spiritual role. Both are essential to the body of Christ.

Paul writes in Ephesians, "And he gave the apostles, the prophets, the evangelists, the shepherds and teachers, to equip the saints for the work of ministry, for building up the body of Christ."[13] The key thought of the Ephesians text is "to equip the saints for the work of ministry for building up the body of Christ."[14] Scriptures are replete with descriptions of shepherds. Some shepherds are good, yet some are bad. Some do God's will, some do not. But if pastors do not do anything to make apprentice disciples, individuals he works with on a one-on-one relationship, they should find those in the church who have the equipper gift and passion. It may be another staff member. Remember, we are the body of Christ. Every member has been gifted to serve the mission of the church. It is essential to understand what Scripture says about spiritual gifts. Romans 12, I Corinthians 12, and Ephesians 4 describe the gifts given to the

Every member has been gifted to serve the mission of the church.

---

12 Luke 18:22 (ESV)
13 Eph. 4:11. (ESV)
14 Ephesians 4:12 (ESV)

members of Christ's church. There are tools which enable Christians to better understand what spiritual gift or gifts they have. Knowing your gifts can be a very freeing experience. They are like a Christian's spiritual job description. Pastors do not have all the gifts for ministry. Isn't it more fun to work as a team in ministry? If they follow the Ephesians 4 text, they will focus on equipping. Pastors who are equippers will equip some to be shepherds. A Pastor does not have to call on every shut-in to be doing the ministry. My wife, as a deaconess, loved this kind of ministry. It fit her gift mix. Every Christian can be equipped for ministry. It is not brain surgery. Pastors who equip others reflect a more visionary role: they see the potential in others when equipping and sharing in ministry.

Pastors and staff members work to make ministry more effective by training others in their gifted areas of service. Pastors who feel they alone can do "real" ministry are not as effective. Why would they try to do it all? It may be a result of pride or ignorance. This is a heart/sin issue. Equipping believers to use their gifts will cause a radical change in ministry. However, it will be worth it. This is critical for the future effectiveness of the church. You do not need to repeat this pastor-centered history.

The history of the Old Testament reveals the heart issue of people. When life is good, many lose sight of Who gave them the blessings of life. *Deuteronomy 31: 20* ESV describes this issue: "For when I have brought them into the land flowing with milk and honey, which I swore to give to their fathers, and they have eaten and are full and grown fat, they will turn to other gods and serve them, and despise me and break my covenant."[15]

---

[15] Deuteronomy 31:20 (ESV)

This passage from Deuteronomy reveals the unholy three at work: Satan, the world, and our flesh. When these forces influence believers, the outcome is spiritual decline. Why don't Christ's followers get this? Could our contentment lead us to resist change? Can Christ's followers ever say everything is fine just the way it is? You should have Holy restlessness. Deuteronomy continues by describing the result of following your own desires: "Many troubles and evils will come upon them."[16] (21)

Clearly God does not cause these "troubles and evils." However, since human beings are sinful by nature, He allows them for educational and humbling purposes. What occurs is our fault, not His.

As I write this, America is undergoing a pandemic of Covid-19 and extreme civil unrest. The nation is divided. Racism and different opinions about wearing protective masks continue to dominate television and social media. In my perception, we are experiencing a wakeup call. Civil unrest is out of control, yet change can occur. It is called repentance.

Repentance is not a feeling like "Sorry I made a mistake." Mistakes are common responses we experience every day. "Oh, I am sorry. I did not mean to step in front of you." Repentance reflects a complete change of direction. It reflects "I am going the wrong way. God forgive me for Jesus' sake. Set me on the better path." "The sacrifices of God are a broken spirit; a broken and contrite heart, O God, you will not despise,"[17] the writer of Psalms says. As disciples, we "rightly divide the Word." (my emphasis)

The Holy Spirit can use the Commandments to hone and sharpen your character so you can share God's Word effectively.

---

[16] Deuteronomy 31:21 (ESV)
[17] Psalms 51:17 (ESV)

If you are not continually growing in your faith, it may be because you are not learning from the scriptures. You may be wilting if not dying. For example, consider the egg plants I am growing on my patio.

If I do not water and feed them fertilizer, they will die. I will not get any fruit. In the same way, Christians need to be fed. On average, approximately 20% of those in worship at my church participate in a regular Bible class. There are many who are spiritually knowledgeable. In fact, one

> *If you are not continually growing in your faith, it may be because you are not learning from the scriptures. You may be wilting if not dying.*

member, who recently died, was a walking Bible. He could cite book, chapter, and verse in the context of our discussions. He was a good friend and model of Christian faith, love, and commitment to a relationship with Christ. However, what about the 80%?

In the Old Testament, Isaiah's picture of God's people is challenging. In chapter 48:1-11 (ESV), he describes the relationship Israel had with the Lord. He describes their confession of God as, "but not in truth or right."[18] Faith had become nothing more than membership in a religious institution.

Isaiah continues his description of the people as those who have "necks like iron sinew."[19] In other words, they were stiff necked. They pretended to be devoted but were only practicing phony religion. He further describes the results. He says they will be refined in the "furnace of affliction."[20] Ask yourself, have we put too many of our "gods" in front of God? Has hedonism taken

---

[18] Isaiah 48:1b (ESV)

[19] Isaiah 48:4b (ESV)

[20] Isaiah 48:10b (ESV)

over? Has the pursuit of pleasure sensual self-indulgence, caused our eyes to be blinded from God? Could this time in history be a season of "furnace of affliction?" Only God knows.

Hardship and trouble can be a good thing. God is changing His Church (universal) which is made up of all believers of different congregations and denominations. History throughout the Old Testament reflects how God intervenes and changes hearts. The challenges and difficulties we face may be the way God opens hearts to the Gospel. In the next chapter we will look at how God confronts our use of His name and how it affects our culture.

CHAPTER TWO

WHAT IS IN A NAME?

"The name above every name."[21]

"You shall not take the name of the Lord, your God, in vain."[22] *What does this mean? Martin Luther said that we should fear and love God so much that we do not curse, swear, use witchcraft, lie, or deceive people by using His name. Instead, we are to call upon Him in every trouble, pray, praise, and give thanks.*[23]

---

[21] Philippians 2:9. (ESV)
[22] Exodus 20:7. (ESV)
[23] Martin Luther, *Luther's Small Catechism. Ibid*

How often have you heard Christian friends using God's name in a flippant and nonchalant manner? Are you shocked, or do you simply ignore it, as though it is acceptable? This is where a follower of Christ can demonstrate a better way. As a response, you can give a counter witness about Jesus as your friend. You do not want others to speak negatively about your friend, Jesus. You should speak up when the time seems appropriate when you first encounter the offense. Ignoring a person's abuse of God's name is often more effective than reacting negatively. In other words, you do not want to cut off communications in the relationship.

One of my favorite descriptions of Jesus' humility comes from Philippians 2:9. It says, "Therefore, God has highly exalted Him (Jesus) and bestowed on him the name that is above every name."[24] There is no other name that God will recognize. He will not respond to our prayers in the name of Tom, Dick, or Harry. It is intentional that Jesus said, "I am the way, and the truth, and the life. No one comes to the Father except through me."[25]

It is amazing how many times throughout the Bible, God's name is used to describe an important event or the relationship with His people. What is in a name that makes it so meaningful? Have you ever experienced a time when a person calls you by a different name other than your own? I have been called Fred instead of Frank. It feels disrespectful. My name is Franklin or Frank. It is the name on my birth certificate. Sometimes I

There is no other name that God will recognize. He will not respond to our prayers in the name of Tom, Dick, or Harry.

---

[24] Philippians 2:9 (ESV)
[25] John 14:6. (ESV)

overlook it when someone butchers my name. Yet it does make me uncomfortable.

Imagine what it must mean to God when His name is used as a curse word. What is it like for Him when His name is used flippantly and without respect? Rather than it being misused, He desires that His name is given as a blessing. Numbers 6:27 (ESV) says, "So shall they put my name upon the people of Israel, and I will bless them." As your name is important and meaningful, so is God's.

"Jesus Christ" is not a cuss word. His name is given for the purpose of salvation. In the New Testament it says, "And there is salvation in no one else, for there is no other name given under heaven among men by which we must be saved."[26]

Another issue occurs from misguided followers of Christ. His name is sometimes used in a political context. Rainn Wilson notes, "The metamorphosis of Jesus Christ from a humble servant of the abject poor to a symbol that stands for gun rights, prosperity theology, anti-science, limited government (that neglects the destitute) and fierce nationalism is truly the strangest transformation in human history."[27]

The name of Jesus is sometimes used in the pursuit of wealth. This is often called the "prosperity gospel." It also is used to fool people into believing they can always be healed of their illnesses. Let us be clear, miracles can and do occur. God's Word says so. I have seen it. It is, however, an act of God's love and mercy when He intervenes on somebody's behalf. However, using the name of Jesus like it is our right to demand something from God is a sin. No one can manipulate God by using His name for personal gain.

---

[26] Acts 4:12. (ESV)

[27] Wilson, Rainn, 2020. Facebook Post, Facebook, August 18, 2020

Name dropping does not work. You cannot gain favor by using God's name for selfish purposes. Health and wealth theology is a gross misuse of God's name. If you could manipulate God, and use His name for all your cures, medical help could be eliminated. No one would need doctors or hospitals. During the COVID-19 pandemic, scientists are working around the clock to find a cure as well as a vaccination. We do not wave a "Jesus' wand" over people and cure them. We do not put blood over our doorpost to ward off plagues as God instructed His people when they were captives in Egypt. We trust God to give us knowledge and scientific skill to get us through this health crises. We use God's Word and His commandments to guide us.

The Ten Commandments need not be burdensome. They are your accuser but turn you to the good news of the cross of Jesus' death and resurrection. In *the Drama of Scripture*, Craig G. Bartholomew describes how the Ten Commandments were used to give God's people the means to know how to live. Those who broke them were stoned. Since America is not a theocracy, we would find this to be a harsh method. However, it does underscore the seriousness of what God's Word means. The Lord says what He means and means what He says. Therefore,

> *The Ten Commandments need not be burdensome. They are our accuser that leads us to the good news.*

His name is so important. His authority, as connected to his name, is not to be flaunted or dismissed as inappropriate for today. Bartholomew says, "The Commandments are thus the keys to living fully human lives; they are certainly not intended as horrible constraints."[28]

---

[28] Bartholomew The Drama of Scripture, Baker Academic page 70

The latter part of what this commandment means, directs believers to praise God's name and give thanks. This concept means we should give thanks in all circumstances, even in times of trouble. Have you ever noticed how your attitude and perspective about a difficult situation changes when you thank God and call upon Him? You see life differently. You are not as discouraged. His name instills a confidence that causes you to praise Him. The Psalmist writes," Oh give thanks to the Lord, for He is good; for his steadfast love endures forever."[29] Another Psalm says, "Rejoice in the Lord, O you righteous, and give thanks to his Holy name."[30] Christ followers who love Him embrace worship in a spirit of truth.

Years ago, I attended a conference in Russia. What a pleasure it was for me to experience God's people worshipping in spirit and truth. Even though they were singing in their own language, there was no doubt Who they were praising. The name of Jesus was being worshipped and adored. They were not just worshipping the name of Jesus, but they were praising Jesus himself. Scripture says, "Where two or three are gathered in his name, Jesus will be there among them."[31]

The first three Commandments describe our relationship with Jesus. The Third Commandment reinforces the first two. You cannot truly worship God if your heart is fixed on the gods of this world. Nor can you effectively apply His name to your circumstances. Your relationship comes together in worship.

---

[29] Psalms 118:29. (ESV)
[30] Psalms 97:12. (ESV)
[31] Matthew 18:20. (ESV)

CHAPTER THREE

WORSHIP

"God is spirit, and those who worship Him must worship in spirit and truth."[32]

"You shall sanctify the Holy day. What does this mean?"

Answer: "We should fear and love God so that we may not despise preaching and His word, but hold it sacred, and gladly hear and learn it."[33]

---

[32] John 4:24. (ESV)
[33] Martin Luther, *Luther's Small Catechism. Ibid*

Scriptures describes God's creation in chapter one of Genesis. In chapter two it says that when God finished His work and on the seventh day, He rested. Most Christians take His seventh day of rest to be a day of worship. Some, like the Seventh Day Adventists, worship on Saturday. The early Church chose Sunday as a day of rest and worship, to remember the day of Christ's resurrection. Roman Emperor Constantine declared Sunday a day of rest on March 7, 321.[34] It has been observed by most followers of Christ ever since.

What is the best form and style for worship? Styles of worship can range from contemporary to traditional. The style is the container, and different styles reflect the heart language of different believers. Like the dementia patient who perks up and smiles when you sing Jesus loves Me. This is their heart language of worship.

Any style can reflect deep or shallow Christianity. Some contemporary services are, "a half inch deep, and a mile wide" in music and message. Some services are dominated by "emotional hype." However, many contemporary styles offer a true and genuine experience.

If the Spirit of Truth is not present in any kind or type of worship, it becomes nothing more than a fruitless act. This applies also to traditional worship. For Christ's followers' worship is a heart language which reflects a relationship with God. In the church it is important that each person find a heart connection with God in spirit and

Some contemporary services are, "a half inch deep, and a mile wide" in music and message.

---

[34] Wikipedia

truth. Christians do not judge one style of worship to be better or more authentic than the other.

Worthship! How much is God worth to you as a follower of Christ? Worship comes from the word" worthship."[35] The substance of worship comes down to relationship. Jesus said, "Whoever has my commandments and keeps them, he it is who loves me. And he who loves me will be loved by my Father, and I will love him and manifest myself to him."[36] If we attend a worship service to be entertained or to satisfy our fleshly desires, it is phony. It is simply lip service. However, if we have a personal relationship with Christ it becomes a joyful and meaningful experience. Examine yourself. Is worship a rote, boring, and monotonous experience?

Are you analyzing and critiquing what the service does and does not include? Why?

Are you expecting the rah, rah kind of service? If you cannot stay focused on the message and meaning in worship and you are focused on going out for breakfast, ask why. Are you analyzing and critiquing what the service does and does not include? Why? Jesus is there! He said, "where two or three are gathered in his name there he would be also."[37]

This commandment reminds believers not to despise or neglect the preaching of God's Word. It reflects our worship attendance. We all need a steady diet. Of course, the key word is God's Word.

This reminds me of a story. There was this farmer who was out plowing his fields. He was a religious man. He looked up in

---

[35] Wikipedia
[36] John 14:21. (ESV)
[37] Matthew 18:20 (ESV)

the sky and saw a cloud formation in the shape of "PC". He got all excited thinking it meant for him to "preach Christ." So, he went to the seminary. He arrived at his first church and began preaching every Sunday. After a few Sundays, the elders of the church gathered with him for a discussion. They asked why he became a preacher. He told them the story about being on the tractor and seeing the cloud formation "PC". He thought it meant to "Preach Christ". One elder spoke up and said, "Pastor, I believe God was telling you to plant corn." If you experience a pastor who is preaching anything but the Word of God, you need to respond. If a preacher focuses on anything but God's Word, that should sound an alarm. Of course, this assumes you have good knowledge of God's Word.

What is the result of empty preaching? Your relationship with Christ may be compromised or hindered. There are many people who have left a church because of a poor or meaningless message. Here is a caution: Do not run from the church. Instead, speak with the pastor. Attempt to offer constructive input. Sometimes it works. Sometimes it does not. In truth, most pastors work hard to prepare a good message. Some are more gifted to do so than others. It is hard work to prepare a meaningful message every week. The most important issue is this: Is the pastor preaching God's Word? Most pastors try to follow the Apostle Paul's words, "For I decided to know nothing among you except Jesus Christ and him crucified."[38]

The *style* of worship is often a controversial issue for American churches. It can sometimes be very divisive. Choosing contemporary worship songs and a less structured format or using hymns and following a traditional liturgical structure can become

---

[38] 1 Corinthians 2:2. (ESV)

an issue. However, worship style should not be the central issue of a church. The aim should always be to proclaim the Gospel of Jesus and welcome the stranger. Is leadership sensitive to others? A church can become so spiritually minded that it is no earthly good. It is best understood when you hear the words from a visitor who says, "nobody greeted me." Failure to offer love, acceptance, and forgiveness to strangers is a sign of "koinonitis", which is a singular emphasis on fellowship among those who already belong to the church. "The unhealthy overemphasis of church member's focus on themselves in an insular, ingrown, self-absorbed body."[39] American Christianity has experienced a crisis in American churches. "The crisis in the U.S. church has almost nothing to do with being liberal or conservative; it has everything to do with giving up on the faith and discipline of our Christian baptism and settling for a common, generic identity that is part patriotism, part consumerism, part violence, and part affluence."[40]

We should pray, "God have mercy! Look kindly upon your disciples and children. Forgive us for Jesus' sake. Teach us again to go to the cross and seek forgiveness. Give us a passion for your commandments."

As mentioned before, the first three Commandments focus on our relationship with Him. The next seven Commandments teach us about our relationships: how we speak, act, and treat one another. The Fourth commandment teaches about how we relate to our parents and authorities.

---

[39] C. Peter Wagner, Discover Your Spiritual Gifts, Baker Books, 2002, 2005, 2012.
[40] Walter Brueggemann, Facebook post, June 17, 2020

CHAPTER FOUR

SPIRITUAL KIDS' STUFF

"Children obey your parents in everything, for this pleases the Lord."[41]

Martin Luther wrote, "You shall honor your father and your mother that it may be well with you and you may live long upon the earth."[42] *What does this mean?*

Answer: "We should fear and love God so that we may not despise or anger our parents and masters, but give them honor, serve them, obey them, and hold them in love and esteem".[43]

---

[41] Colossians 3:20. (ESV)

[42] Ephesians 6:2,3, (ESV)

[43] Martin Luther, *Luther's Small Catechism. Ibid*

My father told me about his childhood. He had an alcoholic father. His father would take him to the local bar and make him sit on a stool while he drank and talked with his friends. Yet, my dad still loved and respected his father. He told me later in life that his longevity, he believed, was due to his conviction about the Fourth Commandment promise, "you may live long upon the earth."[44] My dad lived to be 98 years old. He was a model to me. Colossians 3:20 (ESV) says, it pleases God when we obey our parents.

The reverse role of this commandment reminds me that as a parent I should not frustrate my children through poor parenting. Scripture says, "Fathers, do not provoke your children to anger, but bring them up in the discipline and instruction of the Lord."[45] I cannot expect respect or honor from my children if I act like a dictator. When your child asks "why," and you respond, "because I told you so," it does not communicate well to your child's need. Proverbs says, "Train up a child in the way he should go; ..."[46] The key word is "train." As Jesus modeled and mentored His disciples to maturity, we can follow His example. I must confess I struggle with how my parenting role was perceived by my children. This is likely every parent's concern. Perhaps every parent wishes there were a training manual that came with each child. However, there is

As Jesus modeled and mentored His disciples to maturity, we can follow His example.

one! It is called the Bible. In God's Word we find grace and forgiveness. We can trust Christ's words of assurance. In the last

---

[44] Exodus 20:12 (ESV)
[45] Ephesians 6:4 (ESV)
[46] Proverbs. 22:6. (ESV)

verse of the Great Commission, He promises, "I am with you always."[47] What an awesome God we have!

The second part of the explanation of this commandment deals with honoring those in authority. In the era of the Old Testament, the order of government was a theocracy. It included the Ten Commandments. The religious leaders set up policies, procedures, and behaviors, based on God's Commandments, what the people were to follow. Those in authority were priests and counsels.

In a later period, the people became jealous of their neighbors, who had kings as rulers. The children of Israel rebelled. They too wanted a king to rule over them. I Samuel 8, describes warnings of what a king would do to them. They did not care. They still wanted a king who would fight for them. This was the beginning of authoritarian government.

This use of human authority becomes a present-day challenge for America. How do Christians respond? Paul writes in Romans 13 that all authority has been instituted by God. He explains that the authority has the right to apply the law as well as apply penalties for those who break it. Where does God allow the believer to disregard the law? Anytime the law becomes a license for doing wrong or breaking God's commandments. This will be explained further in chapter five. Romans 13 may seem to imply these passages require blind loyalty to follow the authorities. Many believers might wrestle with this implication. In modern day America, it is often difficult to see those in authority behaving in a civil manner.

So, what are we to do? Bury our heads in the sand? Blindly accept? Absolutely not! The response becomes a mandate for carrying out the Great Commission, to make disciples, followers

---

[47] Matthew 28:20 (ESV)

of Jesus. It begins with prayer for government leaders. Change should always begin with prayer, asking the Holy Spirit to intervene. This approach determines who we trust. People need Jesus Christ. "Civility and respect need to be restored." [48]

Too often the gospel is used as a law. Instead of showing people Jesus and how much He cares for them, they give the impression, "thou must believe." Belief comes by the work of the Holy Spirit's not by your decision. It is a lot more attractive to share a heart of compassion that becomes a witness to those who are lost and confused. Christ followers demonstrate patience and tolerance for all people, including those in authority. Perhaps you have seen street preachers waving their Bibles at people. You might wonder how that type of witness can be effective.

Love, acceptance, and forgiveness works far better to convince people to receive Christ.

Where is the mentoring, the relationship building? Love, acceptance, and forgiveness works far better to convince people to receive Christ. Think about your witness. Is it genuine? Do people want to hear your story? Repentance leads to restoration of our relationship with Christ.

The next chapter focuses on the relationship between attitudes and acts of murder.

---

[48] Kent Hunter, *Restoring Civility self-published*

CHAPTER FIVE

ANGER MANAGEMENT

"You have heard it said to those of old, 'You shall not murder, and whoever murders will be liable to judgement. But I say to you that everyone who is angry with his brother will be liable to judgement."[49]

"You shall not murder."[50] *What does this mean?*

Answer: We should fear and love God so that we may not hurt or harm our neighbor in his body but help and befriend him in every bodily need (in every need and danger of life and body)".[51]

---

[49] Matthew 5:21-21a. (ESV)
[50] Exodus 20:13 (ESV)
[51] Martin Luther, *Luther's Small Catechism. Ibid*

This chapter and the eighth chapter are the most difficult to write. When I go on social media, I often read mean-spirited posts from Christian friends and family. Many have personal opinions about the present political climate. What is my response to many of these posts? It makes me wonder if they know anything about these commandments. Do they know what Jesus taught about being angry? He said, "Everyone who is angry with his brother will be liable to judgement."[52] The contrast of how anger is dealt with is in St. Paul's words found in Ephesians 4: 25-26 (ESV). "Therefore, having put away falsehood, let each one of you speak the truth with his neighbor, for we are members one of another. Be angry and do not sin; do not let the sun go down on your anger."[53] The positive side of dispelling anger is when truth is told. Your Christian response will be to quench lies and not spread misinformation.

It is more disturbing when a president of the U.S. tells those at a rally to "knock the crap out of him" when speaking about a protester at Clinton, Iowa, January 30, 2016. There are some religious people in America who have come to believe this kind of talk and behavior is acceptable. Those in authority have a tremendous amount of influence.

Where has respect and being civil with one another gone? I see this as the failure of many churches across America. They teach Christianity with no Jesus. It is a head thing. I have observed many people grow up in the church, are baptized, taught the catechism, confirmed as members, yet still not follow Jesus. Reminds you of the lesson Jesus taught in Mark, chapter four about the sower.

---

[52] Matthew 5:22 (a). (ESV)
[53] Ephesian 4: 25,26 (ESV)

He is the main source to guide us on the right path. Without Christ our religion is only Christian-ish. The scripture says, "If anyone thinks he is religious and does not bridle his tongue but deceives his heart, this person's religion is worthless."[54] These are strong words—a shock statement. I hope they cause you to think.

Congress cannot pass laws to correct this dilemma. There are already laws on the books for the murder of a person. This is a heart issue. Hate is a killer as much as one person shooting another. Luther's explanation to this commandment calls for Christians to help others with their bodily needs. To befriend those who are mean-spirited friends is a big challenge. So often I have had to stop and bite my tongue before my sinful flesh would blurt out some hateful or mean statement. It could be righteous anger. God only knows. The model to stop me is Christ hanging on the cross. He said, "Father, forgive them because they do not know what they are doing."[55] Grace and forgiveness was poured out from His side for us. The power of Jesus' sacrifice on the cross will change our lives. God's Riches at Christ's Expense is the acronym for grace. There is no law or conditions in Christ's words from the cross. He is looking down at the crowd of the religious elite, the Pharisees and the mockers who have hung Him on the cross. He could call down the power of God's anger on them if he wanted to. Instead, he says "Father forgive them because they do not know what they are doing."[56] The power of Jesus' sacrifice on the cross will change your life. You need

> *Grace and forgiveness poured out from His side for us. The power of the cross will change our lives.*

---

54 James 1:26. (ESV)

55 Luke 23:34. (ESV)

56 Luke 23:34 (ESV)

to spend more time at the foot of the cross. The Holy Spirit invites you to do so. However, it is easier to follow the world and your flesh. "Jesus said, "If anyone would come after me, let him deny himself and take up his cross and follow me."[57]

"There is a big difference, between following Jesus of Nazareth and the political/nationalistic movement that is often called Christianity."[58]. Philip Yancey writes, "C. S. Lewis observed that almost all crimes of Christian history have come about when religion is confused with politics. Politics ... allures us to trade away grace for power, a temptation the church has often been unable to resist." [59]

> "There is a big difference, between following Jesus of Nazareth and the political/nationalistic movement that is often called Christianity." ...

Today, we have, what I call "American Christianity." It is okay for Christians to hate people because they belong to the other party. We justify our hatred because this person did this or that. Judgement and criticism are the norm. Extraordinarily little grace is demonstrated, nor is putting the best construction on the person and their behavior. It is easier to hate than to love and respect. Scripture says, "For I know that nothing good dwells in me, that is in my flesh." [60]

If any of this resonates, you need to know there is forgiveness. It begins with repentance. It ends with absolution. Like Jesus said to the woman at the well, "Go and sin no more."[61] The "mirror" of

---

[57] Matthew 16:24. (ESV)
[58] *The Celtic Christian Tradition*
[59] The Celtic Christian Tradition
[60] Romans 7:18 (a). (ESV)
[61] John 8:11b (ESV)

the law reflects who we are. The grace of Christ reveals who He is. Faith in Christ changes our attitudes and our purpose, and it becomes our guide as His disciple. Instead of hate, we offer love and compassion to the person. It becomes imperative that our witness reveals in whom we trust. Christ crucified and risen from the dead! He is alive!

Instead of hate, we offer love and compassion to the person. It becomes imperative that our witness reveals in whom we trust. Christ crucified.

Simply because the civil law says it is ok to do something it does not always make it right. For example, when civil law causes the Christian to break a commandment it cannot justify murder. For example, abortion is legal. It was made legal in 1973. But it goes against this commandment. Although there are exceptional circumstances which allows the Christian to abort a baby, such as saving the life of the mother, the believer should always seek other means to deal with their baby. Counseling is available. Your pastor will help with this issue. Adoption is a means of helping a couple have a child if they are unable to conceive their own. My grandchildren are all adopted. We love them dearly and are grateful for having them in our family.

Jesus did not excuse ignorance but demonstrated his mercy. He took their place on the cross and in that act provided forgiveness.

What has become normal thinking for many church attenders? How many have chosen to have an abortion? Are they without a conscience? Is there guilt? These are questions that only they can answer. What is your answer?

There is a solution to all these issues. It is found in the word of Christ. "Father forgive them for they do not know what they are doing."[62] Jesus did not excuse ignorance but demonstrated his mercy. He took their place on the cross and in that act provided forgiveness. This forgiveness is for all who have "sinned and fallen short of God's glory."[63] Nobody is perfect, and I am a perfect example. But I do not take my forgiveness for granted. The Bible says, "For the wages of sin is death, but the free gift of God is eternal life in Christ Jesus our Lord."[64] This is our hope and destination. We have a future. We can look forward." Our hope is built on nothing less than Jesus' blood and righteousness."[65]

Chapter six deals with our sexual temptations.

---

[62] Luke 23:34 (ESV)
[63] Romans 3:23. (ESV)
[64] Romans 6:23 (ESV)
[65] Lutheran Worship Hymnal, LW page 368

CHAPTER SIX

SEXUAL DRIFT

"You have heard that it was said, 'You shall not commit adultery.' But I say to you that everyone who looks at a woman with lustful intent has already committed adultery with her in his heart."[66]

"You shall not commit adultery."[67] *What does this mean? Answer: We should fear and love God so that we may lead a pure and decent life in words and deeds, and each love and honor his spouse."*[68]

---

[66] Matthew 5:27-28. (ESV)
[67] Exodus 20:14 (ESV)
[68] Martin Luther, *Luther's Small Catechism*. Ibid

Illicit sex is like a plague in America. Television, Hollywood, books, and strip bars reflect the culture of many. I remember walking down Bourbon Street in New Orleans. Half-nude women swinging on a swing through a window, literally. Women inside were dancing the "hoochie choochy," enticing men. Culture is a powerful force. It can influence an entire country. In the 1940's, America had just come out of a war.

There was an openness to Christianity. America's values were refocused. Many were more receptive to the teaching of God. Church attendance grew in most mainline churches. This was my observation as I grew up. Almost every family on our road went to church. We were good neighbors *Values were built on God's truths.* and helped each other when needed. Values were built on God's truths. Issues like adultery and a promiscuous lifestyle were frowned on and rejected. The church taught these values. They took hold with the members. So, what happened in the last 65 years?

My age group was a part of what was called the Silent Generation. Maintaining a strong foundation of character and responsibility was a strong part of our generation. We were not discontent with the status quo. We wanted to build on what was good and functional. The effects of the war sapped our creativity. So, what happened in the next generation?

The Boomer Generation was born. These were the children of the Silent Generation and the Builders.

Ken Dychtwald, PHD, discusses the Boomer generation in a video commentary The Boomer Century 1964-2064. There were both positive and negative contributions Boomers offered to the culture of America. These also affected churches in America.

Their desire for variety in products and technology boosted the economy. Their ingenuity created many new innovations which is probably their strongest legacy offered. They admired the Ozzie and Harriet lifestyle of a normal family. They fought for and protested the injustices of the institutional systems of America. JFK inspired them with his idealism. His assassination left a big impact on them.

Depending on your perspective, these next contributions may be positive and negative. Educational systems took a more liberal approach toward teaching. Schools taught independent thinking, "listen to your inner voice"- "know yourself". Students were taught to question everything. Even Christianity was challenged. Nothing could stand on its own merits. Everything was up for debate. This resulted in a rebellious generation (as does every generation) who protested the injustices of America. Their music choices became a part of that rebellion.

The hippies were spawned out of this group. A good movie for learning about this generation is *Forrest Gump*. Free sex was unhitched from marriage and became the norm. The birth control pill was invented as a need. Of course, drugs became popular among many. However, the most dramatic change was that many Boomers rejected church. Yet not all of them did. Today America is still a long way from a revival. Many children have followed their parents' misguided path. Thank God for the ones who did not.

> *However, the most dramatic change was that many Boomers rejected church. However, not all of them did. Today America is still a long way from a revival.*

Scripture says, "Let marriage be held in honor among all, and let the marriage bed be undefiled, for God will judge the sexually immoral and adulterous."[69] This verse reinforces the commandment. God is clear about what He expects of believers. His will is that marriage be a lifelong commitment to each other. Husbands and wives are to love, honor, and cherish one another. In the beginning God intended marriage to be a bond of two coming together to become one. "Therefore, a man shall leave his father and his mother and hold fast to his wife, and they shall become one flesh."[70] This bond is not an accident. It is God's plan to create a mirror image of Him and His creation. It is a picture of Christ and the Church, His bride. "So, they are no longer two but one flesh. What therefore God has joined together, let not man separate."[71] If infidelity causes a marriage to end, there is grace and forgiveness for the sinner. It is not a cheap grace, which discounts the price Christ paid on the cross. As stated earlier, repentance should lead us to the foot of the cross. Restoration comes only when the disciple of Christ comes clean. People cannot carry the burden of a failed marriage that is unrepented. Unforgiven sin in a marriage only leads to another bad marriage. Genuine heartfelt repentance frees a couple to see their error and do the right thing. Seek Christian counseling. Focus on God's word. Do not fabricate false justification for why the marriage ended. If a couple reaches an impasse in their marriage and counseling does not work, a separation may be necessary to refocus their marriage. If they cannot reconcile, spiritual counseling is needed to determine who or what they believe. The issue of an unbelieving spouse may justify a reason for divorce, but this is still not God's design.

---

[69] Hebrews 13:4 (ESV)

[70] Genesis 2:24. (ESV)

[71] Matthew 19:6. (ESV)

On the issue of sex, this should be clear. Satan has promoted a big lie. Paul writes in Romans one and two, about gay and lesbian relationships. This sinful condition has existed for as long as history records such cultural conditions. This is not a more egregious sin than any other. However, Paul does not smooth it over as though it is not important. He spends two chapters describing the law, and the difference between righteousness and unrighteousness. He describes specifically what God will do to those who live in this type of relationship. There is no biblical foundation that justifies a homosexual lifestyle. That is another big lie that Satan has promoted in many American churches.

The American "Christian" church likes to remain safe. It wants to keep members happy. "No need to rock the boat with controversial subjects," some say. However, God is the hound of heaven. He does not give up the pursuit of His children. I used to have a beagle hound when I was a young man. I enjoyed rabbit

> *The American "religion" church likes to remain safe. It wants to keep members happy. "No need to rock the boat with controversial subjects," some say.*

hunting. I would take Taffy, my dog, out hunting. She would search in the brush until she smelled a rabbit. Back and forth she would go until she found it. Then the chase was on. She bellowed out her cry letting me know she was on the trail. Rabbits circle when chased. So, I would put myself into the area where Taffy jumped the rabbit and wait for her to bring it around to me. She was relentless. If she temporarily lost the track, she would back track until she found it. She would not give up until she brought the trophy around for me to harvest. It is not a perfect analogy, but it provides a picture of how God loves us. He never gives up until His child responds.

To what extent should churches go to be sure none of the members are lost to this world? Is preaching relevant to the issues of today? Are there law and gospel messages about adultery, homosexuality, the ten commandments? God is serious about these issues, otherwise He would not have given us His word regarding them.

None of these maladies are unforgiveable. Scripture says, "For all have sinned and fall short of the glory of God."[72] There is not one of us who has not sinned, yet every one of us is loved by God. He will not abandon any of His followers, no matter what. His Holy Spirit is gentle. He is not a tyrant. Just when the time is right, God sends His Holy Spirit to bring us to Christ. He leads us to the cross and overwhelms us with such peace and joy. This should be the message of every Christian church in America. "Speak the truth in love."

Chapter seven deals with the commandment about stealing. Another sin that is often justified by worldly influence.

---

[72] Romans 2:23. (ESV)

COMMANDING LIFESTYLE

The Scriptures say, "You know the commandments, 'Do not commit adultery, do not murder, do not **steal**, *do not bear false witness, honor your father and mother".[73]*

"You shall not steal."[74]

What does this mean?

Answer: We should fear and love God so that we may not take our neighbor's money or property, nor get them with bad products or deals, but help him improve and protect his property and business."[75]

---

[73] Luke 18:20. (ESV)
[74] Exodus 20:15 (ESV)
[75] Martin Luther, *Luther's Small Catechism. Ibid*

This commandment reminds me about a man who worked in a wheelbarrow plant. Every day at quitting time he would come to the gate with a wheelbarrow load of sand. The security guard would probe and dig in the sand to be sure the employee was not stealing something. Finally, after several weeks the security guard confronted the employee. "Why are you taking sand out in the wheelbarrow every day?" he asked. The man responded, "So I can steal the wheelbarrow." I know, it is a dumb joke. Yet it is based on a real situation I encountered at a local plant in Fort Wayne, Indiana.

A fellow employee would bring his large thermos bottle of coffee in every day. At the end of the day, he would fill his thermos with small hand tools and other items. He would stuff rags around the items to keep them from rattling. At that time of my life, I was not walking closely with the Lord. I looked the other way even though I knew he was stealing. The attitude of these employees was to think they deserved some fringe benefits from their employer. A study by the Association of Certified Fraud Examiners (ACFE) found that employees often justified their theft with "Corporations don't have feelings." or "No one got hurt." "If my company's going to cut my benefits, it owes me." In 2002, fraud cases like this were found among 16.2% of the workers. By 2018 it increased to 21%. This is a sad indictment of the culture of America. Even more astonishing is that many of these thieves are members of a church.

Does the message of the church address the specific sins or are they generalized? Every follower of Jesus Christ should investigate The Ten Commandments as an important part of their spiritual growth. It was once said that Christians live in glass houses. That is not true in today's culture. Many Christians hide behind the mask of the world and its influence. It is like camouflage used for deer hunting where men blend into the surrounding trees and brush, and they are not seen.

What about the employee who submits an inflated invoice for services they did not accomplish? Or the additional hours they claimed when they had a buddy punch their timecard when they were not even at work. Or what about fraudulent expense reimbursements? Instead of $20 for gas, a worker submits $40. These are just some of the ways the ACFE found fraud.

The fourth chapter of Hosea describes God's accusations against the Israelites. The Lord says there is a controversy among the habitants of the land. They are not faithful, they lack love, and there is little knowledge of God. There is swearing, lying, murder, stealing, and committing adultery.[76] Hosea writes that because of these issues, the land mourns. Ironically, this describes where America is today. Kent Hunter shares the need for a revival of civility. His book, Restoring Civility, offers clarity and precise analysis of this issue. He also describes the solution. "Civility is clarified by clear values, beliefs, attitudes, priorities, and worldviews."[77] If Christian values influence you; they should also be your beacon of witness. Unbelievers also have influence. If Christians promote more of what they are FOR (the Gospel) instead of what they are AGAINST the culture of America can change.

"Civility is clarified by clear values, beliefs, attitudes, priorities, and worldviews."

Jesus started a movement that has continued for generations. His movement is one of changing hearts and attitudes. Those

---

[76] Hosea 4:1b-2a. (ESV)

[77] Kent Hunter, *Restoring Civility*, p. 182.

who encountered Jesus and have followed Him were never the same. His movement was an infectious connection that caused them to leave their vocations and follow him. Fishermen, tax collectors, factory workers, attorneys, and engineers. They all found a different purpose. There would be no return to what was normal. To follow Christ means that nothing is the same anymore. We become "new" creatures, as St. Paul writes.[78]

The explanation of this commandment states that, instead of stealing or using fraudulent methods of gaining your neighbor's property, we should help our neighbor improve his property. Have you ever shoveled your neighbor's sidewalk in the winter? Have you ever helped plant your neighbors garden? Did you ever help build deer hunting towers? (This was my personal contribution to a friend.) The purpose is to help your neighbors retain and improve their property.

> *Jesus started a movement that has continued for generations. His movement is one of changing hearts and attitudes. Those who encountered Jesus and have followed Him were never the same.*

James writes, "But someone will say, 'You have faith and I have works.' Show me your faith apart from works, and I will show you my faith by my works."[79] We should not allow ourselves to be so busy that we have no time to help others.

As shared earlier, I worked for a retail business that cross trained all the employees to know every department. There was another reason. It was a policy to never tell a customer to go to some other department to get their merchandise. Your job was to take them, assist them, and leave them satisfied with your service.

---

[78] 2 Corinthians 5: 17 (ESV)

[79] James 2:18. (ESV)

How does this relate to stealing? If you are sitting and doing nothing to serve the customer, you are stealing from the company and the customer. You are paid to serve, not for chatting with your fellow employee while ignoring the customer. It is all stealing. How often have you encountered cashiers, floor salesman, or loaders ignoring you? They act like you are an inconvenience to them. They act as though it would be better if you did not even come into the store. It is stealing.

This is also a heart/relationship problem. It is difficult for businesses and corporations to legislate behavior. Leaders can model and train until the cows come home, but if an employee's heart is not into service to others it will not matter. Fear of losing your job can be a motivator, but it does not last. Money can sometimes be a motivator, yet it is not sustainable. Successful business leaders know that genuine care and interests in their employees leads to improved motivation and service in the workplace. Annual reviews are not just about their work performance. There needs to be a concern for what is going on with their lives. How are their children? How is their spouse? Do they like their job, and if not, why? This is a relational/heart issue. If a manager discovers an employee is going through a horrendous divorce, it may impact their behavior. If his son or daughter is seriously ill, it could explain a lot.

For the worker motivation becomes a desire to do the right thing. Do not steal from the company. Get counseling and help to deal with your issue. Do not take it out on your employer. Stealing is never a solution. Build a relationship with your employer. The aim is to build character and integrity in relationships. Christ is our mentor.

In Luke 18:20, Jesus summarizes five of the commandments. They all deal with relationships. The rich young ruler was looking for an easy road to eternal life. Jesus catches him in his hypocrisy and challenges him to give up all he owned and says, "Come follow me."[80] The relationship always takes precedent over the rules. Jesus showed the young ruler the importance of a relationship with him. The rich young man boasted that he kept all those commandments. However, he missed the point. Jesus says, "I am the way, the truth, and the life ..."[81] faith in Jesus is not a religion that is Christian-ish but a life changing relationship. That is Jesus' message to us. "Come follow me."[82] It requires dedication, commitment, and sacrifice. There is no easy road to eternal life or service in God's kingdom. You may even find yourself being attacked by members of your own congregation. I was assaulted by a member for serving the black people of the community. Yet, it is all joy. Life is never the same once you are in a relationship with Jesus.

---

[80] Luke 18:20 (ESV)
[81] John 14:6 (ESV)
[82] Luke 18:22b (ESV)

CHAPTER EIGHT

THE POWER OF YOUR MOUTH

"The one who conceals hatred has lying lips, and whoever utters slander is a fool."[83]

"You shall not bear false witness against your neighbor."[84]

What does this mean?

Answer: "We shall fear and love God so that we may not deceitfully belie, betray, slander, or defame our neighbor, but defend him, think and speak well of him, and put the best construction on everything." [85]

---

[83] Proverbs 10:18. (ESV)
[84] Exodus 20:16 (ESV)
[85] Martin Luther, *Luther's Small Catechism. Ibid*

Defamation of character is the legal term used when someone has slandered or verbally lied or mischaracterized someone. It can occur in a speech, a sermon, a TV ad, or any discussion about another person. When America was in the middle of an election for president and many congressional seats, this past year, there was not much truth in the TV ads. Liable occurs when someone mischaracterizes or lies about someone in a written form or in a document. Examples include messages shared on Facebook, Twitter, public posters, or ads. It amazes me how this has become so acceptable with no consequences.

It is my observation that some Christians violate this commandment intentionally. They know it is wrong to speak or write badly about others, yet it occurs often. A brief look at social media reveals this violation. For me, this is the hardest issue to get my head around. Social media spreads so many lies and conspiracies. It sometimes seems like no one cares about facts or the truth when they post. If someone posts a conspiracy about something bizarre, something strange, very few people check it out. Many believed it as truth. Posts are blasted out with little thought about how they could mislead others. So many people give no thought to how this reflects on their *These posts are like skunk urine, which repels rather than invites.* Christian witness. These posts are like skunk urine, which repels rather than invites. These issues are one of the reasons this book about the American "Christianity" has been written. Often, the shocking statements family members or friends put on social media cause me grief. The mirror of God's Law reveals how far Christians have gotten out of line. So many no longer are seeing this as a commandment that should guide them.

A post I saw on social media accurately describes the "American Christianity". My definition of "American Christianity" "Having the appearance of godliness but denying its power."[86] It says, "As for me and my house, we will: 1) salute the flag and stand for the National Anthem, 2) kneel before the cross, and 3) serve our Lord."[87] This is in great contrast to Joshua twenty-four verse fifteen.

> "And if it is evil in your eyes to serve the Lord, choose this day whom you will serve, whether the gods your fathers served in the region beyond the River, or the gods of the Amorites in whose land you dwell. **But as for me and my house, we will serve the Lord."**[88]

This is the choice Christians face today. The American flag is not a Christian's first priority. Beliefs and values are key to the way believers communicate. Values and beliefs begin at an early age. Your worldview determines much of what is most important. If you get your beliefs, values, and worldviews from your friends at the bar, you are in the wrong cultural environment. Bar conversations may be good for discussions about basketball and football. However, politics and religion are

Beliefs and values are key to the way believers communicate. Values and beliefs begin at an early age. Your worldview determines much of what is most important.

---

[86] 2 Timothy 3: 5 (ESV)

[87] Facebook post Sunday June 7, 2020, Tony D. Krukow, Hollister, MO

[88] Joshua 24:15 (ESV)

frequently abused. The atmosphere could be a soap box for Satan to mislead you as a Christian.

Pastors need to speak to the issues people face today. Their sermons must reflect a balance of law and gospel. Many pastors use sermon guides with biblical themes. However, few of them focus on current issues people face every day. Issues related to the Eighth Commandment should be incorporated into their preaching messages. It may require some discipline, but it is needed. People need to know what God says and apply it to our daily challenges. Speaking negatively or writing lies about your neighbor results from a sinful desire of selfishness. It is tempting to want others to look bad so we can look good. Selfish ambition is part of your sinful nature. Paul writes, "Do nothing from selfish ambition or conceit, but in humility count others more significant than yourselves. Let each of you look not only to his own interests, but also to the interests of others."[89]

Your commitment to others can go one step further. In chapter 18, Matthew encourages Christ's followers to discuss issues that has caused an offense. If a lie has been spoken about another person, seek reconciliation. Peace can only occur through a heartfelt dialogue. This happens when Christ is present in the relationship between two people. It requires a surrender to God of both pride and will. The model for this is Christ Himself.

It amazes me how Christ in His humility was totally committed to his Father's will. Can you imagine Christ saying to His Father, this cup is too much to bear …? I cannot go to the cross for the sins of the people. "Salvation is for people to figure out on their own." How absurd would that be? Instead, He said, 'Father if you

---

[89] Philippians 2:3,4. (ESV)

are willing, remove this cup from me. **Nevertheless, not my will, but yours be done** [Emphasis added]."[90]

Jesus' purpose was salvation for all people. He knew, without doubt, His life was the only way people would have forgiveness of their sins against others. Jesus is the bridge between all relationships.

The cross was His destination for us. This was for your forgiveness. His resurrection is for your destination of eternity. What an awesome God we worship! Ponder on His act of love.

The second part of the explanation for this commandment says, "defend your neighbor, think, and speak well of him, and to put the best construction on everything."[91] To approach your neighbor in a positive way may take different forms. If you learn that someone is having marital problems, offer support and provide a listening ear. Their anger toward others may be a diversion from difficulties

> *Jesus' purpose was salvation for all people. He knew, without doubt, His life was the only way people would have forgiveness of their sins against others. Jesus is the bridge between all relationships.*

with their spouse. Perhaps you have heard this: "If momma ain't happy, there ain't nobody happy." The point? Find the source of their anger and help them discover a remedy.

Be prepared to recognize that the person may not be reachable at this time. A better approach may be to pray for them. Commend them to God, asking the Holy Spirit to work in their heart. It will help you from thinking ill of the individual. Prayer helps to refocus.

---

[90] Luke 22:42. (ESV)
[91] Martin Luther, Luther's Small Catechism, ibid

Consider this: How often do pastors or members use the Ten Commandments as a guide for prayer? Have you ever used them in that way? You might find it to be a helpful plan.

Here is another approach. "Martin Luther wrote a little book on prayer for his barber, Peter. In it, he lays out his simple method of praying Bible verses. It is brilliant. I call it "I.T.C.P":

- Instruction
- Thanksgiving
- Confession
- Prayer

The method anchors prayer in the texts of Scripture or the catechism but allows the Holy Spirit to prompt thoughts via the Word, which may be chased more freely by the mind at prayer...

Luther explains his method, using the Ten Commandments:

"I think of each commandment as, first, *instruction*, which is really what it is intended to be, and consider what the Lord God demands of me so earnestly. Second, I turn it into a *thanksgiving*; third, a *confession*; and fourth, a *prayer*. I do so in thoughts or words such as these: "I am the Lord your God, etc. You shall have no other gods before me," etc. Here I earnestly consider that God expects and teaches me to trust Him sincerely in all things and that it is His most earnest purpose to be my God...

Second, I give thanks for His infinite compassion by which He has come to me in such a fatherly way and, unasked, unbidden, and unmerited, has offered to be my God, to care for me and to be my comfort, guardian, help, and strength in every time of need. We poor mortals have sought so many gods and would have to seek them still if He did not enable us to hear Him openly tell us in our own language that He intends to be our God. How could we ever—in all eternity—thank Him enough!

Third, I confess and acknowledge my great sin and ingratitude for having so shamefully despised such sublime teachings and such a precious gift throughout my whole life, and for having fearfully provoked His wrath by countless acts of idolatry. I repent of these and ask for His grace.

Fourth, I pray and say: "O my God and Lord, help me by Thy grace to learn and understand Thy commandments more fully every day and to live by them in sincere confidence. Preserve my heart so that I shall never again become forgetful and ungrateful, that I may never seek after other gods or other consolation on earth or in any creature, but cling truly and solely to Thee, my only God. Amen, dear Lord God and Father. Amen"[92]

Luther's advice to his barber, Peter, is brilliant. You can pray verses from the Bible, Christian songs, statements of faith, catechism, and other resources. Start with the Ten Commandments!

The Eighth Commandment is timely in the history of America today. The gospel cannot be buried under a blanket of cultural garbage. The good news of Jesus is our focus. The Ninth Commandment deals with coveting your neighbor's possessions. The glitter of this world is extremely attractive. In the next chapter we will discuss how this Commandment is appropriate currently.

---

[92] Matthew Harrison, *Luther's Works*, 43:200.

CHAPTER NINE

POSSESSED BY POSSESSIONS.

"And He (Jesus) said to them, take care and be on your guard against all covetousness, for one's life does not consist in the abundance of his possessions."[93]

"You shall not covet your neighbor's house."[94]

What does this mean?

Answer: We should fear and love God so that we may not craftily seek to get our neighbor's inheritance or house or obtain it by a show of justice and right, or any other means, but help and be of service to him in keeping it."[95]

---

[93] Luke 12:15. (ESV)

[94] Exodus 20:17a (ESV)

[95] Martin Luther, *Luther's Small Catechism. Ibid*

The world, our flesh, and Satan make everything attractive, "something we just got to have." Perhaps you have heard people say that when they see something they would like to possess; "covet, covet, covet." Perhaps it is a statement said in jest. Yet it describes the nature of our sinful desire. This is not to say you should not desire to get a new house. If that desire becomes an obsession which leads to breaking the First Commandment, your desire becomes coveting. Jesus said we should guard against all forms of covetousness. Value in life is not based on possessions. However, values and beliefs often determine what we deem most important. As Christians we value God's Word and our relationship with Jesus most of all. His commandments are the guide that keeps us "walking" with the Lord. I grew up in Indiana where Canadian thistles are abundant. When I was child, I learned a lesson about thistles. It is about how something attractive can lead to a bad outcome. Canadian thistles have an incredibly beautiful and attractive blue flower. A large field of them is a marvelous site. Just as a television ad about a new car can be enticing, the blue flowers of thistles can also be attractive. One day, I decided to pick some of those beautiful blue flowers. I would be a good son and take them home to my mom. It did not take me long to figure out that I was in a heap of hurt. They are nasty and very painful. The point is this: Our natural inclination is to desire something; however, it may not be good for us. Some things are more subtle than an encounter with thistles.

Our natural inclination is to desire something; however, it may not be good for us. Some things are more subtle than an encounter with thistles. Satan is tricky and deceitful. Yet, there is a good side to curiosity.

Satan is tricky and deceitful. Yet, there is a good side to curiosity. God created us with a curiosity for discovering the beauty of His creation. It was the beauty of the fruit in the garden that attracted Adam and Eve into sin. Our curious nature is only bad when our sinful nature causes us to covet. Curiosity drives us to learn. It also causes us to want more. Marketers appeal to that part of our nature to entice us to buy things.

Marketing has numerous strategies. The first is to establish your target audience. Some focus on the elderly. A grandchild helps grandpa figure out how to use the new television. Other ads deal with products that help with walking aids. Different ethnic groups become target audiences.

As Christians we value God's Word most of all. His commandments are the guide that keeps us "walking" with the Lord.

Children are targets. Do you remember the jingle, "N E S T L E S, Nestles makes the very best chooocolate?"

A second strategy of marketing focuses on telling you the product is believable. This assumes you know how to discern truth and can tell the difference. Is it real or a fabrication that does not make sense? The object of ads is to create something nonsensical. They are intended to make you remember the product. The challenge with these ads is you may not know what they are selling. You just remember the silly ad.

The third strategy of advertising is to appeal to your senses. Are you attracted to it? Do you feel you absolutely need this product? I confess I would like a new Rav 4, but, thanks to my wife, she keeps me in line. Our present automobile has only 52 thousand miles on it. So why would I need a new car? My covetous nature!

The central point of the Ninth Commandment is this: If your desire for what belongs to somebody else leads you to connive or use dishonest means, you are already trapped by sin. Do you know families who take their own brothers and sisters to court to lay claim to the family inheritance? Or neighbors who take a piece of property away from their neighbor to use as a driveway? This was my father's personal experience.

> The apostle Paul addresses this dilemma. "When one of you has a grievance against another, does he dare go to law before the unrighteous instead of the saints? Or do you not know that the saints will judge the world? And if the world is to be judged by you, are you incompetent to try trivial cases? Do you not know that we are to judge angels? How much more, then, matters pertaining to this life! So, if you have such cases, why do you lay them before those who have no standing in the church? I say this to your shame. Can it be that there is no one among you wise enough to settle a dispute between the brothers, but brother goes to law against brother, and that before unbelievers? To have lawsuits at all with one another is already a defeat for you. Why not rather suffer wrong? Why not rather be defrauded? But you yourselves wrong and defraud—even your own brothers!"[96]

In your church would you hear a message preached based on that text? It does not appeal to itchy ears. The purpose here is not

---

[96] 1 Corinthians 6:1-8. (ESV)

to assault churches. However, this is a cultural condition, and it requires a prophetic voice. America needs to wake up! Across the United States, Christians often experience apathy. Safe sermons and Bible classes frequently keep the believer comfortable. Sound biblical law and gospel messages must be preached about the real issues in the culture of America. The author of Hebrews wrote about this message, "For by this time you ought to be teachers, you need someone to teach you the basic principles of the oracles of God. You need milk, not solid food. For everyone who lives on milk is unskilled in the word of righteousness since he is a child."[97] In other words, scriptures tell us to grow and mature as Christians. The Word offered is at your fingertips. Use it to proclaim the Christ of Scriptures.

I recently heard a pastor on television say, "If America will see a revival, there must be repentance." To simply feel sorry for your sins is just the beginning. Repentance is a complete change in direction. If coveting, lying, adultery, idolatry, and any of the other Commandments have a specific message of conviction for you, repent. "A burning wick He (Christ) will not snuff out."[98] Jesus accepts us with open arms. He will never deny any of us the forgiveness of sin. He would betray Himself if He did. His death on the cross would be useless. God's work on the cross with His Son was to offer grace and mercy in abundance. Nobody is exempt or denied from grace. If you reject it, that is your fault not God's.

God's work on the cross with His Son was to offer grace and mercy in abundance. Nobody is exempt from grace.

---

[97] Hebrews 5:12-13. (ESV)
[98] Isaiah 42:3 (ESV)

This reminds me about another concept about grace. I believe we all have what I call a grace measuring stick. It is a stick we use to measure how far we go before we have gone too far into sin. In other words, a little sin is okay as long as we do not go beyond our measuring stick. It is okay to cuss when it seems appropriate. We can ask for forgiveness for this. It is not all that egregious. A drinking habit is not all that bad as long as I can still act normal. You get the point. We all have a grace measuring stick.

Receive His grace and forgiveness. Confess your pet sins, give your measuring stick a toss in the fire. God's grace responds in the breath of a prayer. That prayer could be, "Father thank you for sending your Son to be our Savior and Brother. Forgive us for His sake and restore us to be advocates and ambassadors who share His love with others. Amen."

CHAPTER TEN

DESTROYING IDOLS

"Put to death therefore what is earthly in you: sexual immorality, impurity, passion, evil desire, and covetousness, which is idolatry."[99]

"You shall not covet your neighbor's wife, or his manservant, or his maidservant, or his cattle, or anything that is his."[100]

What does this mean?

Answer: "We should fear and love God so that we may not turn, force, or entice away our neighbor's wife, servants, or cattle, but urge them to stay and carefully do their duty."[101]

---

[99] Colossians 3:5. (ESV)

[100] Exodus 20:17b (ESV)

[101] Martin Luther, *Luther's Small Catechism. Ibid*

Interestingly, Paul writes in Colossians that covetousness, sexual immorality, impurity, evil desire, and passion are all forms of idolatry. In other words, these all break the First Commandment. Desiring anything, a person's spouse, his livestock, or anything is a sin.

Without question relationships crumble when one partner or the other finds themselves admiring somebody else's spouse. It may start as an innocent meeting or encounter. They discuss some issue with which they both identify. One issue leads to another, and they start getting serious about a relationship. They have begun coveting. They look for more ways to get together. Unless someone intervenes, or unless one of them comes under a conviction that what they are doing is sin, divorce lies ahead or adultery.

This scenario has become so common, many inside the church accept it as normal. Why? What causes believers to become so calloused that this becomes an acceptable sin? No one wants to "rock the boat" or "make waves." "It is not my problem," as George Forman says in a commercial. We simply mind our own business. Paul writes to the Galatians, in chapter six, "Brothers, if anyone is caught in any transgression, you who are spiritual should restore him in a spirit of gentleness. Keep watch on yourself, lest you too be tempted."[102] We have an obligation to our brother or sister in Christ. It is not a popular issue, but it may be the best thing for fellow believers. It is important that we hold each other accountable.

The key words are, "you who are spiritual."[103] That does not refer only to the pastor. If that is what Paul meant he would have

---

[102] Galatians 6:1 (ESV)
[103] Galatians 6:1b (ESV)

said, "you pastors who are spiritual." Disciples or apprentices of Christ are also able to counsel a friend. You may be the only person who can help. Embarrassment often prevents church members from going to their pastor. It may even cause them to leave the church. Part of ministry is to be sensitive care givers to one another. Follow- up with fellow members is essential to prevent lost children of God.

Divorce statistics are alarming. Statistics for 2019 indicate that first marriages have a 42-45 percent chance of termination. Second marriages have 60 % likelihood at failure. Third marriages have 73% chance of ending. Twenty two percent of first marriages will end in five years or less. Thirty three percent will last ten years or less. Data is produced from independent resources and the US census and the Canterbury Law Group. This is a snapshot of how alarming American culture has become. Unfortunately, in many other countries it is as bad or worse. "American Christianity" is not going to change the culture. It is part of the issue. Repentance and revival, brought about with law and gospel, can lead to renewed civility.

Paul writes, in the letter to the Colossians, "to put to death that which is earthly."[104] What does this mean? Look at Paul's words to the Romans[105]

> "Likewise, my brothers, you also have died to the law through the body of Christ, so that you may belong to another, to him who has been raised from the dead, in order that we may bear fruit for God. For while we were living in the flesh, our

---

[104] Colossians 3:5 (ESV)
[105] Romans 7:4-6. (ESV)

sinful passions, aroused by the law, were at work in our members to bear fruit for death. But now we are released from the law, having died to that which held us captive, so that we serve in the new way of the Spirit and not in the old way of the written code."[106]

Those who have been baptized, have been baptized into Christ's death and resurrection. We put to death our old nature daily when we consciously remember our baptisms. Our relationship with Christ assures us of forgiveness, hope for eternal life and security. The only occasion when coveting is not a sin is when we covet our relationship with Christ. Covet means to want ardently or have something, especially what another person has.[107] In this case we yearn to have Christ and His gift of salvation and the forgiveness of sins. Another

> *Our relationship with Christ assures us of forgiveness, hope for eternal life and security. The only occasion when coveting is not a sin is when we covet our relationship with Christ.*

synonym of covet is to pant after something or someone. I have a tattoo on my shoulder of a deer drinking from a stream of water. The verse under it says, "As a deer pants for flowing streams, so pants my soul for you, O God."[108]

When a Christian is tempted to covet, there is a choice. It can be a positive choice to seek after Christ, as He reminds us the ninth and tenth Commandments, or a negative choice to follow your flesh. The world throws temptations at you every day. Television

---

[106] Romans 7:4-6 (ESV)

[107] Webster's New World Dictionary Fourth Addition

[108] Psalm 42:1. (ESV)

is an entertainment center as well as an exposure to the manure that it often promotes. Again, you have choices. If Christians are growing in maturity (sanctification) through regular Bible study, they know what choices to make. God's Word gives a clear path to follow. The Commandments are not scary when we use them to examine ourselves. They become beacons of encouragement. "The Ten Commandments are good news." … "The commandments are thus the keys to living fully human lives; they are certainly not intended as horrible constraints to make life difficult."[109]

American churches are in transition. The Pandemic of 2020 totally interrupted the normal way of doing church. The way churches worship, conduct meetings, and Bible classes changed. Congregations had to develop a new normal. Most had to experiment and test new ways to do church. In the process it has become certain that the body of Christ will be renewed and revived. Let us hope that churches become a university of disciple makers. Pray that they are no longer an institution but living organism reflecting the body of Christ.

---

[109] Bartholomew, *The Drama of Scripture.*

SUMMARY

This journey has been a very humbling experience. Each chapter reveals how much I fall short of living the truth of each of the Ten Commandments. It also makes me realize how I fail at fulfilling the purpose of the Church—the Great Commission. I cannot make excuses or fabricate reasons to justify this failure. But I am convinced that Christ forgives me and gives me hope and a destiny. God has molded me through various trials and hardships. I am living with prostate cancer. Three years ago, I was told I would probably be dead by now. Perhaps God fooled the doctor. The Lord has guarded me from death on several other occasions. I had pneumonia as a child, hundreds of bee stings over my entire body, ingestion of poison ivy leaves that resulted in blisters everywhere, cancer, and a heart attack. He has made it clear to me that He has a purpose for me. He is the central reason I am convinced this book is appropriate and needed at this time in America.

America and other countries have a cultural compulsion for protesting everything. Recently we have observed peaceful protests. Some of the protests have helped change America. Protests accomplish some lasting effects. But I am convinced there must be a better way.

I am convinced that if American Christians would have been standing up for what they are _for_ instead of what they are _against_ churches would be vibrant and alive, making disciples. "We are not called to fill the pews with members, we are called to fill the world with disciples."[110] Instead of American churches acting Christian-ish pray there would be a contagion of Biblical Christianity -- a body of Christ so attractive, like bees to nectar. I can only imagine. Would it not be amazing?

We are living at a time when American churches must reinvent what will become a new normal ministry. We will not go back. Normal does not exist. We cannot continue in greed, selfishness, lying, cheating, slandering, immoral behavior, and expect God to bless us. We have a spiritual heart issue. Repentance is the only resolution for this condition. One cannot say I love Christ and at the same time slander your neighbor. The two are not compatible. The church's present witness is often perceived as meaningless to the world's nonbelievers. The **alternative** is found in St Paul's letter to the Corinthians. He writes,

> "You yourselves are our letter of recommendation, written on our hearts, to be known and read by all. And you show that you are a letter from Christ delivered by us, written not with ink but with the Spirit of the living God, not on tablets of stone but on tablets of human hearts."[111]

This is the church's witness.

Luke describes what disciples should be doing. It is what you are for, not what you are against. "When they preached the **gospel** to that city (Derbe) and made many disciples, they returned to Lystra and to Iconium and to Antioch, strengthening the souls of the disciples, encouraging them to continue in the faith, and

---

[110] Stacy L. Sanchez, Facebook post. August 2020
[111] 2 Corinthians 3:2,3. (ESV)

saying that through many tribulations we must enter the **kingdom of God**. [Emphasis added]"[112]

What might be the tribulation for America? It seems many Christians live cushy and protected lives. Why? Because we are so earthly minded that we are not Kingdom people, a people whose devotion should be given to The King of Kings, The Lord Jesus Christ. I admit kingdom thinking is difficult.

Kent Hunter in his book, *Who Broke my Church*, discusses kingdom culture. He mentions other nations like the UK, Turkey and others that are earthly kingdoms. The issue about kingdoms is they have one who dictates what the rules of government are to be. God's Kingdom is not a rule of government but a family of people who look to Him for guidance. As simple as it sounds, there are two kinds of people in the world. There are those in God's kingdom and those who are not. Our mission, with the guidance of the Holy Spirit, is to persuade and invite those who are not disciples to become disciples, making them Kingdom members. America has become one of the largest mission fields in the world. I would like to say we are still a Christian nation, but it is difficult to prove.

> *God's Kingdom is not a rule of government but a family of people who look to Him for guidance.*

The call to the American church; all denominations, is to repent. What kind of ministry do Christians want the world to see? The church will embrace a form of worship and fellowship that is inviting and relevant to our new culture. The church is going to change because God is changing it.

---

[112] Acts 14:21-22. (ESV)

As a believer, learn to go with the leading of the Holy Spirit. Look where God is working and join Him. Expect joy and peace beyond measure. Expect to see a civil cultural change. Expect to see love, acceptance, and forgiveness. Life cannot remain as it has been. God will not allow it. History has shown that God does not let His people go without intervention. He is changing the church. **It begins with you.**

DISCUSSION QUESTIONS

Introduction

1. What does the Hebrew writer mean when he says believers "ought to be teachers"? (Hebrews 5:12 ESV)

2. How does discernment, (the ability to recognize good from evil) work in the body of Christ's Church?

3. What is your purpose in ministry?

4. What is your church's purpose?

5. Are you satisfied with your church's methods of equipping members to serve in ministry? What would make it better?

Chapter One

1. If you were to do a spiritual health check of your church, on a scale of one to five, with five being the most healthy, how would you rate your church? And why?

2. How often do you evaluate the specific actions or disciplines you use to grow in your faith and mission?

   a) besides mere church attendance?
   b) in light of the Ten Commandments?
3. How does the Spritual gifts that God has given you, contribute to the purpose of the church? What are your gifts?

4. Does your pastor actively train and equip apprentice disciples for ministry? What actions or methods does he use to do this?

Chapter Two

1. Does it bother you when name of Jesus is used or abused in an inappropriate way?

2. Does your lifestyle reveal how important Jesus' name is for you?

3. How does being "Christian" set you apart from the world?

4. How do attitudes affect your behavior and how you speak?

5. How are attitudes formed?

Chapter Three

1. Do worship styles affect attendance at a church? Why? Or Why not?

2. If worship is a heart language and connection with God, should there only be one form? Why? Or Why not?

3. The central focus of worship is The Triune God. However, it is important to also welcome the stranger. Evaluate how effective your church is at this.

4. What is Koinonitis? Do you agree or disagee that koinonitis is a problem that should be avoided?

Chapter Four

1. Each generation develops a worldview of authority. How does your worldview affect your behavior toward authority?

2. Should the church have affect on government? Why or why not?

3. Do your prayers include the government officials? For what should we, as disciples pray?

4. How do your actions connect directly to the spread of the Gospel? What you are _for_ or what you are _against_?

Chapter Five

1. When is anger ok or a good thing?

2. How do you determine if your anger is ok or motivated by sin?

3. What spiritual ability determines how you know the difference between good and evil?

4. What makes it easy to trade grace for power?

Chapter Six

1. Is America a Christian nation? Why? Or Why not?

2. Have you heard sermons directed at the culture of America? How may they be helpful?

3. Are sermons more generic about sins rather than specific about the Ten Commandments? What message causes you to say ouch?

4. Discuss ways your generation has been affected by American culture.

Chapter Seven

1. When you take a pen and don't return it is that stealing?

2. How do your attitudes get formed about what determines stealing or other behaviors?

3. What satisfaction do you get when you help a friend or neighbor maintain or improve their property?

4. Is playing a game on your computer, while at work, stealing?

Chapter Eight

1. How do you know when someone is lying?

2. Is slander acceptable? Define its meaning. When or why? Why not?

3. Values and worldviews shape behaviors. How do they affect the church?

4. How do praying through the Commandments help with controling your tongue?

Chapter Nine

1. What does contentment have to do with your Christian's witness?

2. Do you believe Television ads? Why or Why not?

3. What means do you use to grow up in faith?

4. In the book, it describes a grace measuring stick. Discuss some of your pet sins if your willing.

Chapter Ten

1. Is it ok to admire another's spouse? Why or why not?

2. What determines coveting? Or when does admiring something or someone cross over into coveting?

3. When seeing your friend behaving wrongly toward another's spouse what would you do?

4. When is coveting ok?

Summary

1. What does it mean to stand for something instead of against something?

2. Is the church changing? And should it change?

ABOUT THE AUTHOR

Certified as a Commissioned Minister of Religion, from The Lutheran Church Missouri Synod (LCMS), served as a "Lay Minister". Graduated from Concordia Lutheran College, Mequon, Wisconsin formerly Milwaukee. Educated at The University of West Florida, UWF with bachelor's degree in communications.

Frank Grepke is an Evangelist whom God has used to introduce many to Jesus. He is a churchman who has led spiritual movements in the marketplace, as well as on staff in churches in Michigan, Indiana, and Florida. Grepke has served key roles at Church Doctor Ministries. He has also taught pastors in Nigeria, West Africa and introduced Jesus to a nursing staff at a hospital in Moscow, Russia. Grepke's passion is to help biblical churches reach the lost people for Jesus.

Printed in the United States
by Baker & Taylor Publisher Services